Can You See?

Level 4 – Blue

Helpful Hints for Reading at Home

The graphemes (written letters) and phonemes (units of sound) used throughout this series are aligned with Letters and Sounds. This offers a consistent approach to learning, whether reading at home or in the classroom.

HERE IS A LIST OF PHONEMES FOR THIS PHASE OF LEARNING. AN EXAMPLE OF THE PRONUNCIATION CAN BE FOUND IN BRACKETS.

Phase 3			
j (jug)	v (van)	w (wet)	x (fox)
y (yellow)	z (zoo)	zz (buzz)	qu (quick)
ch (chip)	sh (shop)	th (thin/then)	ng (ring)
ai (rain)	ee (feet)	igh (night)	oa (boat)
oo (boot/look)	ar (farm)	or (for)	ur (hurt)
ow (cow)	oi (coin)	ear (dear)	air (fair)
ure (sure)	er (corner)		

HERE ARE SOME WORDS WHICH YOUR CHILD MAY FIND TRICKY.

Phase 3 Tricky Words			
he	you	she	they
we	all	me	are
be	my	was	her

Phase 4 Tricky Words			
said	were	have	there
like	little	so	one
do	when	some	out
come	what		

TOP TIPS FOR HELPING YOUR CHILD TO READ:

- Allow children time to break down unfamiliar words into units of sound and then encourage children to string these sounds together to create the word.

- Encourage your child to point out any focus phonics when they are used.

- Read through the book more than once to grow confidence.

- Ask simple questions about the text to assess understanding.

- Encourage children to use illustrations as prompts.

This book focuses on /igh/ and /ar/ and is a Blue level 4 book band.

Can you sort all the words on this page into two groups?

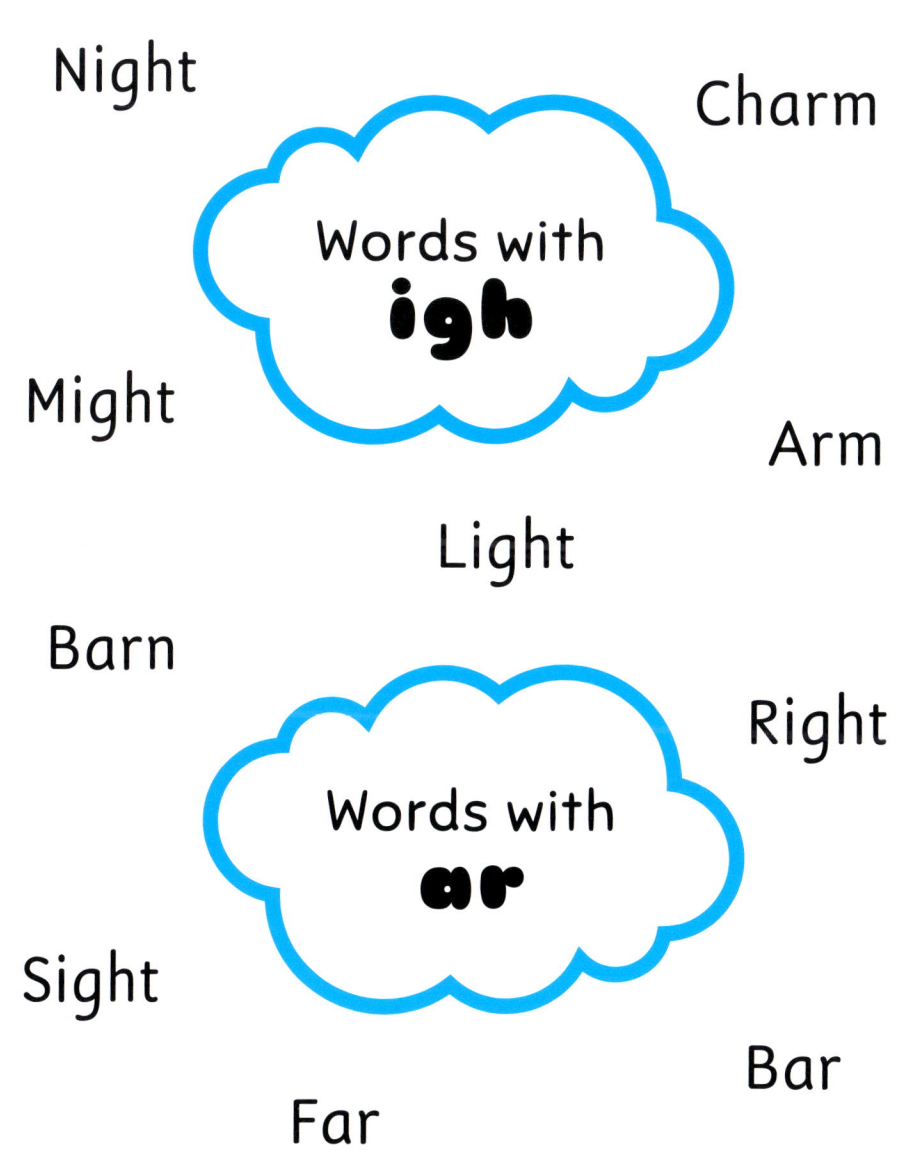

Night

Charm

Might

Arm

Light

Barn

Right

Sight

Bar

Far

You can get a test to understand how well you can see.

They will point a bright light at you.
It cannot harm you.

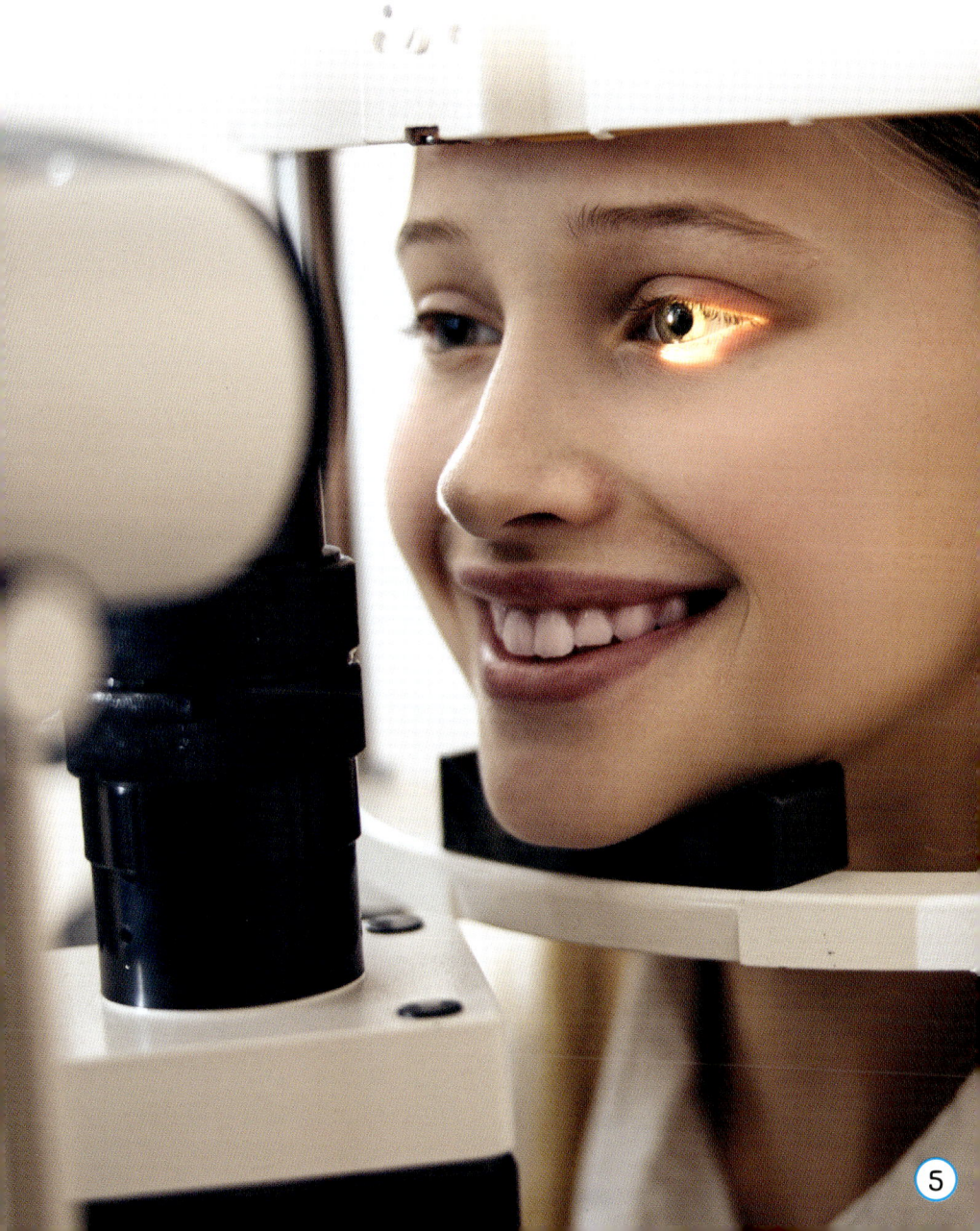

The chin rest will help you see the right spot.

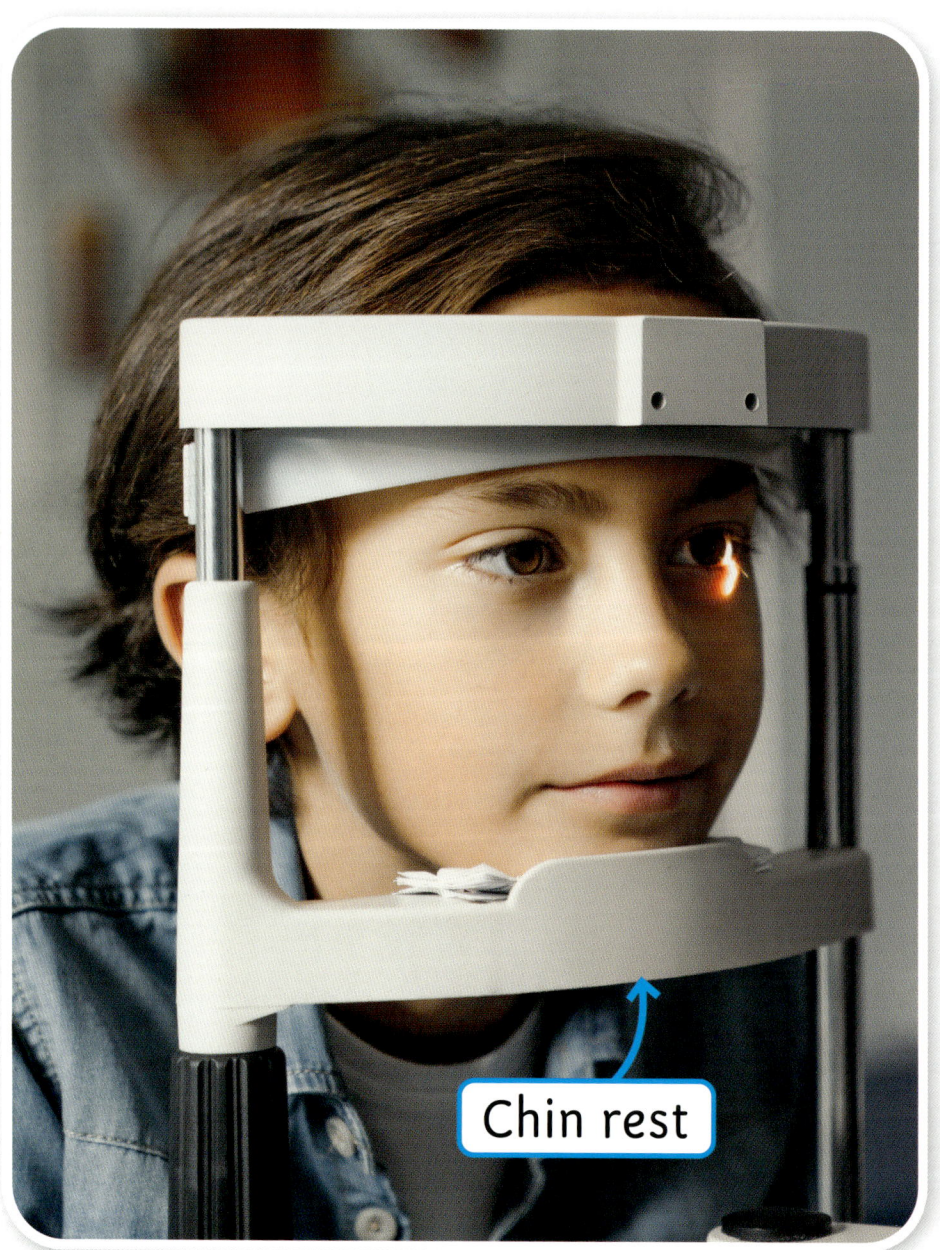

Chin rest

They might have a chart up for you to look at.

Chart

Can you see a big letter at the top?

Can you see the little letters? Some might be hard to see.

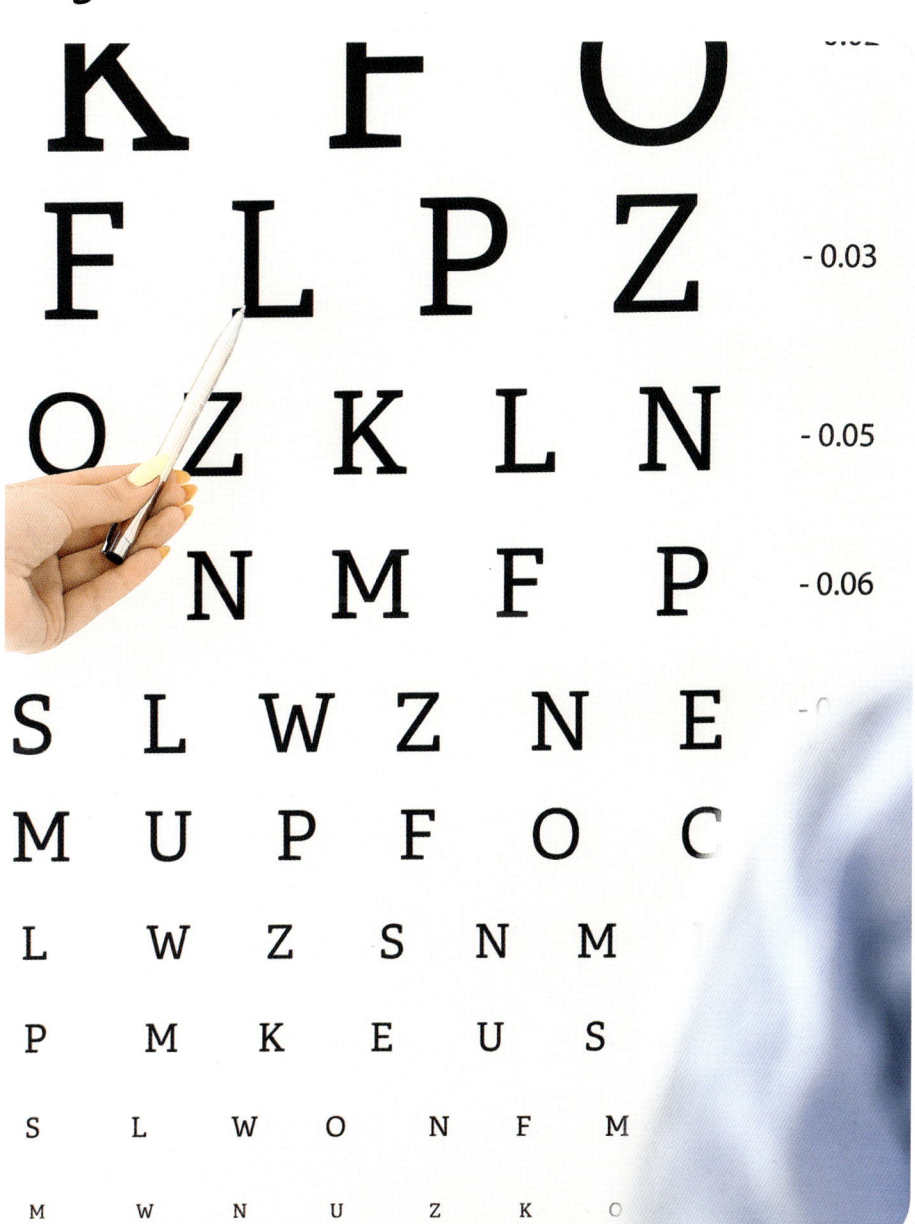

If you cannot see some letters,
you might need help to see better.

You might need to look at the letters with a lens.

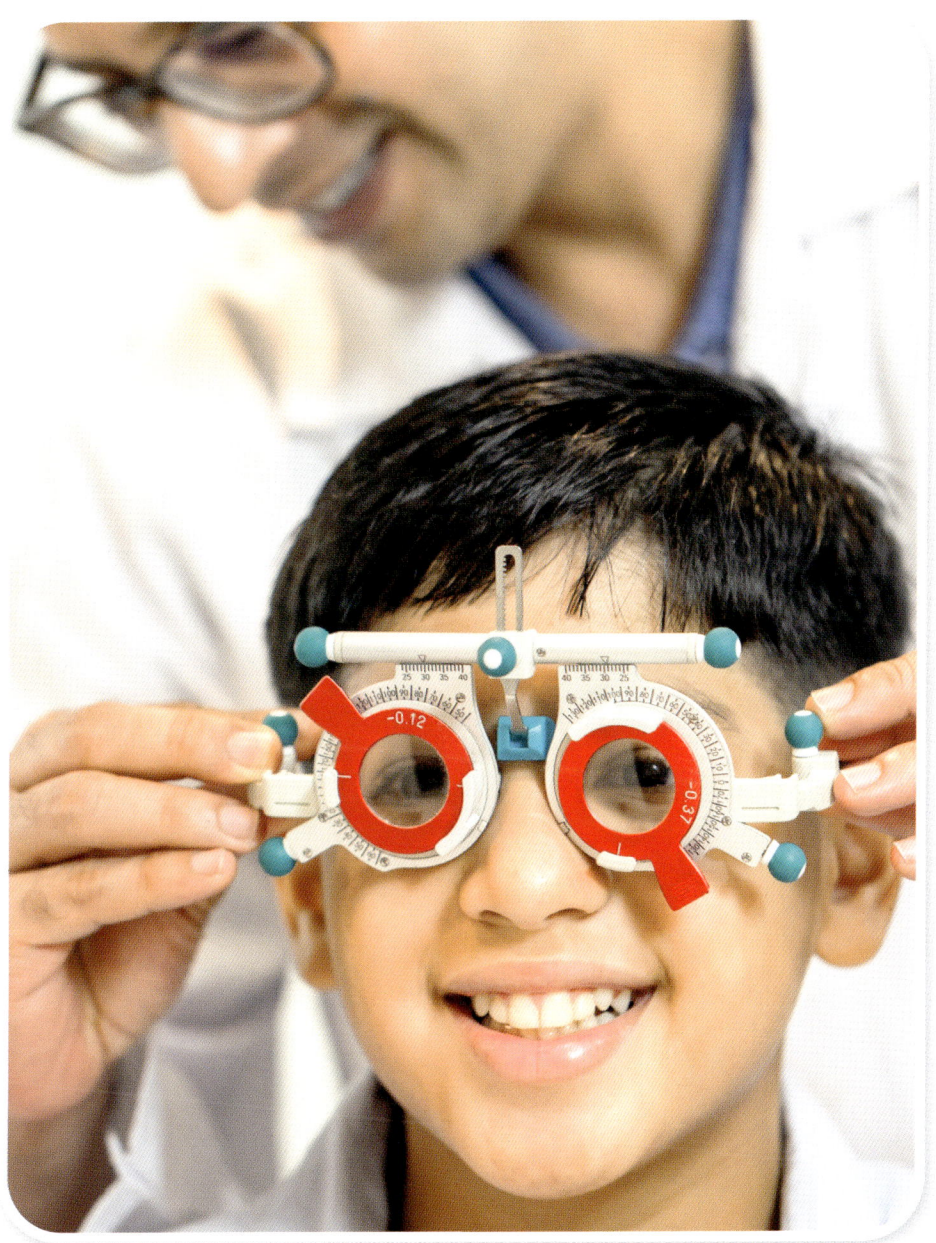

If you can see well with the lens, they might get you glasses.

This part is an arm. This part is the rim. This part is a lens.

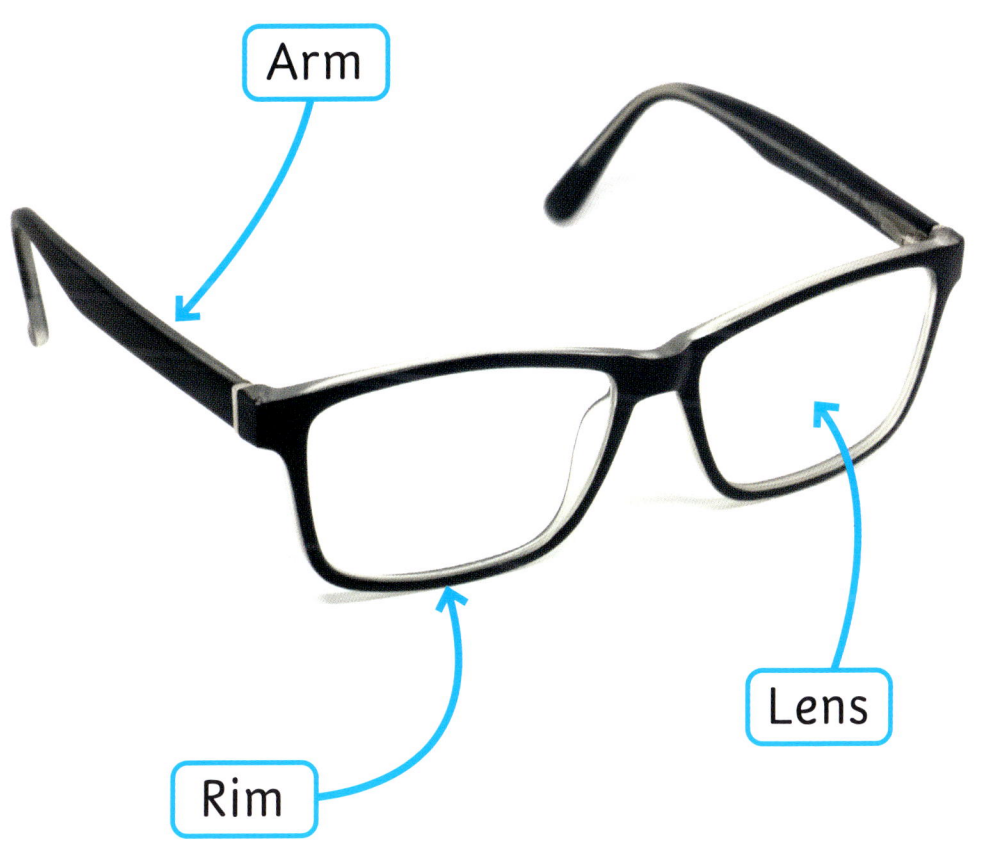

If you do need them, glasses will help you to see better.

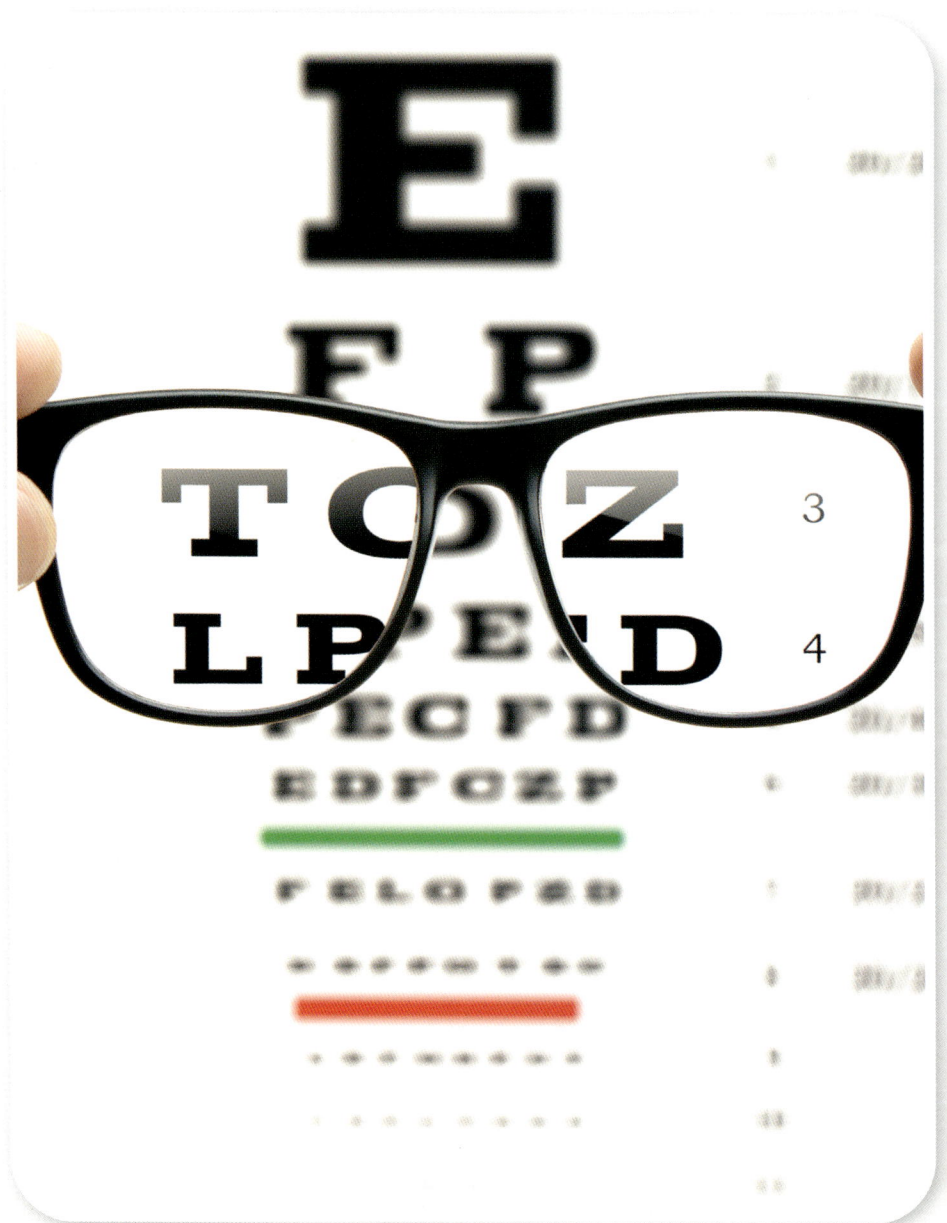

Glasses can help you see things that are near and far better.

©2023 **BookLife Publishing Ltd.**
King's Lynn, Norfolk, PE30 4LS, UK

ISBN 978-1-80505-050-6

All rights reserved. Printed in China.
A catalogue record for this book is available from the British Library.

Can You See?
Written by Charis Mather
Designed by Jasmine Pointer

MIX
Paper from responsible sources
FSC® C113515

An Introduction to BookLife Readers...

Our Readers have been specifically created in line with the London Institute of Education's approach to book banding and are phonetically decodable and ordered to support each phase of Letters and Sounds.

Each book has been created to provide the best possible reading and learning experience. Our aim is to share our love of books with children, providing both emerging readers and prolific page-turners with beautiful books that are guaranteed to provoke interest and learning, regardless of ability.

BOOK BAND GRADED using the Institute of Education's approach to levelling.

PHONETICALLY DECODABLE supporting each phase of Letters and Sounds.

EXERCISES AND QUESTIONS to offer reinforcement and to ascertain comprehension.

CLEAR DESIGN to inspire and provoke engagement, providing the reader with clear visual representations of each non-fiction topic.

AUTHOR INSIGHT:
CHARIS MATHER

Charis Mather is a children's author at BookLife Publishing who has a love for reading and writing. Her studies in linguistics and experiences working with young readers have given her a knack for writing material that suits a range of ages and skill levels. Charis is passionate about producing books that emphasise the fun in reading and is convinced that no matter how much you already know, there is always something new to learn.

PHASE 4
/igh/
/ar/

This book focuses on /igh/ and /ar/ and is a Blue level 4 book band.

Image Credits Images are courtesy of Shutterstock.com. With thanks to Getty Images, Thinkstock Photo and iStockphoto. Cover – leungchopan, Hryshchyshen Serhii, Murad Ahmadli, vectortatu. 4–5 – Dmytro Zinkevych, Svitlana Hulko. 6–7 – Inside Creative House, leungchopan. 8–9 – CandyBox Images, Pixel-Shot. 10–11 – Gatot Adri, JU.STOCKER. 12–13 – Ground Picture, Brylynskyi. 14–15 – rangizzz, Tewcaps.